Contents
Grammar, Punctuation & Spelling: Year 6

Contents	Page
Introduction	
About this book	4
Advice for parents and carers	5
Advice for children	6
Test coverage table	7
Tests	
Test A	10
Test B	33
Test C	57
Marks & guidance	
Marking and assessing the papers	81
Mark schemes for Test A	**83**
● Paper 1: Questions	83
● Paper 2: Spelling test script	86
Mark schemes for Test B	**89**
● Paper 1: Questions	89
● Paper 2: Spelling test script	93
Mark schemes for Test C	**96**
● Paper 1: Questions	96
● Paper 2: Spelling test script	100

C000258415

About this book

This book provides you with practice papers to help support children with the Key Stage 2 Grammar, Punctuation & Spelling test.

Using the practice papers

The practice papers in this book can be used as you would any other practice materials. The children will need to be familiar with specific test-focused skills, such as reading carefully, leaving questions until the end if they seem too difficult, working at a suitable pace and checking through their work.

About the tests

Each Grammar, Punctuation & Spelling test for Year 6 has two parts:

- a short-answer Grammar, Punctuation and Vocabulary test, lasting 45 minutes
- a spelling test lasting around 15 minutes (although this is untimed).

This book provides three different tests and mark schemes.

The script for the spelling task for each paper can be found towards the end of the book.

GRAMMAR, SPELLING AND PUNCTUATION

SATs TESTS

YEAR 6

SCHOLASTIC

Book End, Range Road, Witney, Oxfordshire, OX29 0YD

www.scholastic.co.uk

© 2018 Scholastic Ltd

123456789   8901234567

A British Library Cataloguing-in-Publication Data
A catalogue record for this book is available from the
British Library.

ISBN 978-1407-18297-1

Printed and bound by Ashford Colour Press

All rights reserved. This book is sold subject to the condition that
it shall not, by way of trade or otherwise, be lent, hired out or
otherwise circulated without the publisher's prior consent in any
form of binding or cover other than that in which it is published
and without a similar condition, including this condition, being
imposed upon the subsequent purchaser.

No part of this publication may be reproduced, stored in a
retrieval system, or transmitted, in any form or by any means,
electronic, mechanical, photocopying, recording or otherwise
without the prior permission of the publisher. This publication
remains copyright.

Author

Lesley Fletcher

Series consultants

Lesley and Graham Fletcher

Editorial team

Rachel Morgan, Tracey Cowell, Anna Hall,
Rebecca Rothwell, Sally Rigg, Shelley Welsh and Liz Evans

Design team

Nicolle Thomas, Neil Salt and Oxford Designers and Illustrators

Cover illustrations

Istock/calvindexter and Tomek.gr / Shutterstock/Visual Generation

Acknowledgements

Extracts from Department for Education website ©
Crown Copyright. Reproduced under the terms of the
Open Government Licence (OGL). www.nationalarchives.
gov.uk/doc/open-government-licence/version/3/

Every effort has been made to trace copyright holders
for the works reproduced in this publication, and the
publishers apologise or any inadvertent omissions.

Advice for parents and carers

How this book will help

This book will support your child to get ready for the KS2 National Grammar, Punctuation & Spelling tests commonly called SATs. It provides valuable practice of content expected of Year 6 children aged 10–11 years.

In the weeks (and sometimes months) leading up to the National Tests, your child will be given plenty of practice, revision and tips to give them the best possible chance to demonstrate their knowledge and understanding. It is important to try to practise outside of school and many children benefit from extra input. This book will help your child prepare and build their confidence and their ability to work to a time limit. Practice is vital and every opportunity helps, so don't start too late.

In this book you will find three Grammar, Punctuation & Spelling tests. The layout and format of each test closely matches those used in the National Tests, so your child will become familiar with what to expect and get used to the style of the tests. There is a comprehensive answer section and guidance about how to mark the questions.

Tips

- Make sure that you allow your child to take the tests in a quiet environment where they are not likely to be interrupted or distracted.

- Make sure your child has a flat surface to work on, with plenty of space to spread out and good light.

- Emphasise the importance of reading and re-reading a question, and to underline or circle any important information.

- These papers are similar to the ones your child will take in May in Year 6, and they therefore give you a good idea of strengths and areas for development. When you have found areas that require some more practice, it is useful to go over these again and practise similar types of question with your child.

- Go through the tests again together, identify any gaps in learning and address any misconceptions or areas of misunderstanding. If you are unsure of anything yourself, then make an appointment to see your child's teacher who will be able to help and advise further.

Advice for children

What to do before the test

- Revise and practise on a regular basis.
- Spend at least two hours a week practising.
- Focus on the areas you are least confident in to get better.
- Get a good night's sleep and eat a wholesome breakfast.
- Be on time for school.
- Have all the necessary materials.
- Avoid stressful situations before a test.

SCHOLASTIC National Curriculum SATs Tests

Test coverage table

Paper 1: Grammar, Punctuation & Vocabulary: Year 6

The children will need to be familiar with and be able to demonstrate use of the following.

	Content
Grammatical words and word classes	Nouns
	Verbs
	Adjectives
	Conjunctions
	Pronouns Possessive pronouns Relative pronouns
	Adverbs Adverbials Fronted adverbials
	Prepositions
	Determiners
	Subjects Objects
Functions of sentences	Statements Questions Exclamations Commands
Combining words, phrases and clauses	Sentences Clauses
	Noun phrases
	Co-ordinating conjunctions Subordinating conjunctions Subordinate clauses
	Simple past and simple present tense Verbs in the perfect form Modal verbs Present and past progressive tense Tense consistency
	Subjunctive verb forms Passive Active

	Content
Punctuation	Capital letters Full stops Question marks Exclamation marks
	Commas in lists Commas to clarify meaning Commas after fronted adverbials
	Inverted commas
	Apostrophes for contraction Apostrophes for possession
	Punctuation for parenthesis
	Colons Semi-colons Single dashes Hyphens Bullet points
Vocabulary	Synonyms Antonyms Prefixes Suffixes Word families
Standard English and formality	Standard English Formal and informal vocabulary Formal and informal structures The subjunctive
Partially assessed	Paragraphs Headings Subheadings

Grammar, Punctuation & Spelling

Test A

Grammar, Punctuation & Spelling

Test A, Paper 1: Questions

Questions and answers

You have 45 minutes to complete this paper. There are different types of question for you to answer in different ways. The space for your answer shows you what type of answer is needed. Write your answer in the space provided.

- **Multiple choice answers:** for some questions you do not need to do any writing. Read the instructions carefully so you know how to answer the question.

- **Short answers:** some questions are followed by a line or a box. This shows you need to write a word, a few words or a sentence.

Marks

The number of marks in the margin tells you the maximum number of marks for each question.

You should work through the paper until you are asked to stop.

Work as quickly and as carefully as you can. If you finish before the end, go back and check your work.

You will have 45 minutes to answer the questions in this paper.

1. Use the correct **punctuation mark** in these sentences.

Marks

| ! | ? | . |

It is a sunny day ☐

What a sunny day ☐

When is it going to be sunny ☐

1

2. Underline the three **determiners** in the sentence below.

The dragon went to a cave and blew out some

enormous flames.

1

3. Underline all the **adjectives**.

The frost glistened like chilly, white icing.

The sea lapped lazily onto the soft, golden sand.

1

4. Circle all the words in the sentence below that should start with a **capital letter**.

princess elizabeth married her husband, philip of greece,

in november 1947 in london.

1

5. Which sentence uses **inverted commas** correctly?

Marks

Tick **one**.

Look at all that mud! exclaimed Mum. "You really need to dry the dog when you bring her in." ☐

"Look at all that mud! exclaimed Mum." You really need to dry the dog when you bring her in. ☐

"Look at all that mud!" exclaimed Mum. "You really need to dry the dog when you bring her in." ☐

"Look at all that mud!" exclaimed Mum. You really need to dry the dog when you bring her in. ☐

1

6. Write the best **pronoun** to replace the underlined words.

| ours | we | yours | theirs | us | mine |

<u>Your dad and I</u> will increase your pocket money next month.

[ ]

My pencil's gone. May I borrow <u>your pencil</u>?

[ ]

1

7. Underline the **main clause** in this sentence.

Despite eating a healthy diet, many people still suffer from heart disease.

1

8. Circle the **possessive pronoun** which shows the pen belongs to you.

That's not Jack's pen, it's _____.

| mine | ours | my |

Marks

1

9. Tick the sentence which must end with a **question mark**.

Tick **one**.

They wondered how they had arrived so early ☐

What a surprise to see you so early ☐

You have arrived early, haven't you ☐

Their early arrival surprised everyone ☐

1

10. Which sentence below is written in the **present perfect**?

Tick **one**.

Our village holds a summer fete every year. ☐

Our village has held a summer fete this year. ☐

Our village is holding a summer fete this year. ☐

Our village had held a summer fete in previous years. ☐

1

Marks

11. Which of the sentences below is a **command**?

Tick **one**.

Before drying the dishes, you will need to wash them. ☐

When you go out, remember to take your coat. ☐

I want you to post these letters this morning. ☐

You must learn these spellings by next week. ☐

1

12. Which **pair of verbs** correctly complete this sentence?

Dinosaurs _____ displayed in the British Museum but they _____ alive during the Jurassic Period.

Tick **one**.

is	are	☐
was	were	☐
are	were	☐
is	was	☐

1

13. Circle the **punctuation mark** which should go in the box. Circle **one**.

At the far side of the river ☐ we could see a kingfisher.

,	.	!	?

1

Marks

14. Choose the same **suffix** to change these **adjectives** to **adverbs**. Rewrite the new words in full in the space provided. You may need to change some letters.

ness	ly	er

careful _____

quick _____

mysterious _____

happy _____

1

15. Write these words as **contractions**.

cannot _____

would not _____

I will _____

we are _____

1

16. Choose an **antonym** to replace the word in bold.

A **grotesque** crone staggered slowly towards the archway.

_____

1

17. Use each of those **prefixes** to make new words. Rewrite the new words in the space provided.

Marks

| re | dis | un | in |

respect   _____

appropriate   _____

produce   _____

attractive   _____

1

18. Rewrite this sentence, making the **subject** and **verb** agree.

Amy and Jack goes to the cinema each Monday.

_____

1

19. a. Write in **all** the missing **commas**.

The harvest basket was full of apples oranges pears and bananas.

1

b. Why are **commas** needed in the above sentence?

Tick **one**.

To avoid ambiguity. ☐

To separate speech from the rest of a sentence. ☐

To take the place of brackets. ☐

To separate items in a list. ☐

1

Marks

20. Which option correctly introduces the **subordinate clause** in the sentence below?

Ohmid still wanted to go the theatre _____

it was fully booked.

Tick **one**.

furthermore ☐

in addition ☐

since ☐

even though ☐

1

21. Join and rewrite these sentences using a different **conjunction** in each sentence.

| because | when | if |

They had a wonderful holiday.

The weather was hot and sunny.

_____

_____

Ahmed and Sunita will be very cold.

They do not wear their coats.

_____

_____

1

Marks

22. Circle all the **prepositions** in these sentences.

New Year is celebrated after Christmas.

The match was abandoned because of the fog.

The explorers discovered America during the

fifteenth century.

1

23. Rewrite the sentences, putting **apostrophes** in the correct place.

They were thrilled by the two boys diving display.

_____

The teams goal caused an uproar.

_____

1

24. Write the missing **punctuation** in the box.

| . | ; | : | ... |

Near the reef, there was a great variety of marine

life manta rays, stingrays, turtles and even baby sharks!

1

SCHOLASTIC National Curriculum SATs Tests

Marks

25. Add a **subordinate clause** to this sentence.

We went to the park _____

1

26. Which of the events in the sentences below is **most** likely to happen?

Tick **one**.

We could go shopping this morning. ☐

She might bake a cake this afternoon. ☐

They will go to the cinema this evening. ☐

He might eat sandwiches for lunch. ☐

1

27. Underline the **relative pronoun** in the sentence below.

The film that we saw was very exciting.

1

28. What does the root <u>circu</u> mean in the **word family** below?

circumference   circumnavigate   circumstance   circulate

Tick **one**.

about ☐

in ☐

round ☐

travel ☐

1

Marks

29. Tick **one** box in this sentence to show the correct place to use a **semi-colon**.

The flight ☐ was very long and arduous ☐ it was a relief ☐ when we landed.

1

30. Look at this passage.

When choosing a holiday destination, you need to consider many things. First, you need to think about your budget and decide which destinations match it. You must plan for the interests and needs of all your party. After all that, you still need to decide if the climate and travelling time for your chosen destination are appropriate.

Tick **all** the statements which describe the passage.

It is written in the past tense. ☐

It uses commas to clarify meaning. ☐

It uses several adjectives. ☐

It uses adverbials to order the text. ☐

It is written in the present tense. ☐

It uses commas to separate items in a list. ☐

1

31. When choosing a holiday destination, you need to consider many things. First, you need to think about your budget and decide which destinations match <u>it</u>.

Marks

Draw a line to match the **pronoun** <u>it</u> to the **noun** it replaces in the passage above.

Pronoun

it

Noun

budget

holiday

destinations

1

---

32. <u>After all that</u>, you still need to decide if the climate and travelling time for your chosen destination are appropriate.

<u>After all that</u> is used as:

Tick **one**.

a noun phrase. ☐

a preposition. ☐

a conjunction. ☐

an adverbial phrase. ☐

1

33. Some of the **punctuation** is missing in the text below. Insert the correct punctuation into each of the spaces.

Marks

Everything happened so quickly ☐ a swirl of brown,

a whirl of white and the sausages flew out of sight ☐

Who could have done it ☐

1

34. Rewrite the sentence below as direct speech. Remember to punctuate your sentence correctly.

They asked if she wanted to come to the party.

They asked her, _____

1

35. Tick one box in each row to show the correct type of each underlined **adverb**.

Sentence	Adverb of time	Adverb of place	Adverb of possibility
We were <u>soon</u> able to reach the summit.			
They would <u>surely</u> reach the summit before night.			
If they kept moving <u>forwards</u> they would reach the summit.			

1

■SCHOLASTIC National Curriculum SATs Tests

36. I really enjoyed watching the show (<u>though it was very long</u>) and the acting was magnificent.

Marks

a. Circle the name of the **punctuation** outside of the words <u>though it was very long</u>.

| colon | commas | brackets | dashes |

1

b. Why is this **punctuation** used in the sentence above?

Tick **one**.

It is used instead of colons. ☐

It is used to separate additional information. ☐

It is used to separate a description. ☐

It is used to show speech. ☐

1

37. Circle the **relative pronouns** in the sentences below.

Jack, who was very hungry, went home for tea.

The goal, which the opposing team scored, was an own goal.

1

38. Draw a line to match each word to its **antonym**.

Marks

decrease		scarce
valuable		kind
malicious		increase
abundant		worthless

1

39. Tick the sentence which uses the **subjunctive form**.

Tick **one**.

I wish I was on holiday. ☐

I wish I had gone on holiday. ☐

I wish I were on holiday. ☐

I wish I was going on holiday. ☐

1

40. a. Tick the correct **question tag** for this sentence.

Children always work hard for tests, _____

Tick **one**.

don't I? ☐

aren't they? ☐

are you? ☐

don't they? ☐

Marks

1

b. Explain why **question tags** are used.

_____

_____

1

41. Join each sentence to the correct label.

I ain't giving you any.

You cannot have anything.

Informal speech

Would you please pass me the cake.

Formal speech

Gimme the cake.

1

Marks

42. Add a **colon** to improve the clarity of this sentence.

The performance includes a famous folk singer, the local brass band, an enthralling magician and a cheeky ventriloquist.

1

43. a. Write a sentence with the word <u>judge</u> as a **noun**. Remember to punctuate your answer correctly.

_____

1

b. Write a sentence with the word <u>judge</u> as a **verb**. Remember to punctuate your answer correctly.

_____

1

44. Rewrite the sentences, changing them from the **active voice** to the **passive voice**. One has been done for you.

Active voice	Passive voice
The bird ate the nuts.	The nuts were eaten by the bird.
Jamal read his book.	
The theatre put on a great show.	

1

SCHOLASTIC National Curriculum SATs Tests

45. In this passage, five words have been underlined. In the table below the passage, tick one box in each row to show the **type of word**.

Marks

The <u>overdue</u> bus crawled up the hill. Its engine was old, weary and ready for replacement. As <u>it</u> neared the bus stop, great gusts of <u>steam</u> <u>rose</u> up from <u>under</u> its red, rain-splashed bonnet.

Word	Pronoun	Adjective	Verb	Preposition	Noun
overdue					
it					
steam					
rose					
under					

2

End of paper

Grammar, Punctuation & Spelling

Test A, Paper 2: Spelling

Instructions

- Your **spelling** will be tested in this paper.

- **20 short sentences** will be read aloud to you. A single word has been missed out of each sentence and you need to write this in the space provided.

- **You will hear each word three times.** The word will be said once, then read within a sentence, then repeated a third time. You should write the spelling in the space provided.

- All 20 sentences will be read again at the end, when you will be able to make any changes you wish to what you have written down.

- This paper should take approximately **15 minutes** to complete, although you will be allowed as much time as you need to complete the task.

1. Amy ———————— watching football on television.

2. His ———————— got the better of him and he began to open the parcel.

3. The audience was ———————— for a long time after the final bow.

4. Ellie ———————— chickenpox from one of her friends.

5. We need to ensure we pack all the ———————— medications.

6. Oscar ———————— enthusiastically to the teacher's question.

7. Most novels have a good and a bad ————————.

8. Many famous people write an ———————— which goes on sale just before Christmas.

9. Sometimes, it can be difficult to know which ———————— to watch on television.

10. An ———————— polygon does not have equal sides or angles.

Test A, Paper 2: Spelling

11. Rashid missed the bus _____ he might have caught it if he had left earlier.

12. Use your _____ to help you create an exciting adventure.

13. Painting the _____ was a long and difficult job.

14. There are _____ ceremonies on 11 November every year.

15. The _____ on Friday was below zero.

16. Our _____ are very friendly.

17. After a collision in netball, Jamilla received a large _____.

18. Use a _____ to help you spell tricky words.

19. My dad was _____ on Monday.

20. We _____ go to see my grandparents.

End of paper

Question		Focus	Possible marks	Actual marks
Paper 1	1	Punctuation: punctuation marks	1	
	2	Grammar: determiners	1	
	3	Grammar: adjectives	1	
	4	Punctuation: capital letters	1	
	5	Punctuation: inverted commas	1	
	6	Grammar: pronouns	1	
	7	Grammar: clauses	1	
	8	Grammar: possessive pronouns	1	
	9	Punctuation: question marks	1	
	10	Grammar: present perfect	1	
	11	Grammar: commands	1	
	12	Grammar: verbs	1	
	13	Punctuation: commas	1	
	14	Grammar: adverbs	1	
	15	Punctuation: apostrophes	1	
	16	Vocabulary: antonyms	1	
	17	Vocabulary: prefixes	1	
	18	Grammar: verb tenses	1	
	19	Punctuation: commas in lists	2	
	20	Grammar: clauses	1	
	21	Grammar: conjunctions	1	
	22	Grammar: prepositions	1	
	23	Punctuation: apostrophes	1	
	24	Punctuation: colons	1	
	25	Grammar: clauses	1	
	26	Grammar: modal verbs	1	
	27	Grammar: relative pronouns	1	
	28	Vocabulary: word families	1	
	29	Punctuation: semi-colons	1	
	30	Grammar: commas, adverbials, present tense	1	
	31	Grammar: pronouns	1	
	32	Grammar: fronted adverbials	1	
	33	Punctuation: colons, exclamation marks, question marks	1	
	34	Punctuation: direct speech	1	
	35	Grammar: adverbs	1	
	36	Punctuation: brackets	2	
	37	Grammar: relative pronouns	1	
	38	Vocabulary: antonyms	1	
	39	Grammar: subjunctive form	1	
	40	Grammar: question tags	2	
	41	Grammar: formal and informal	1	
	42	Punctuation: colons	1	
	43	Grammar: nouns and verbs	2	
	44	Grammar: active and passive voice	1	
	45	Grammar: word classes	2	
Paper 2	1–20	Spelling	20	
		Total	**70**	

Grammar, Punctuation & Spelling

Test B

Questions and answers

You have 45 minutes to complete this paper. There are different types of question for you to answer in different ways. The space for your answer shows you what type of answer is needed. Write your answer in the space provided.

- **Multiple choice answers:** for some questions you do not need to do any writing. Read the instructions carefully so you know how to answer the question.

- **Short answers:** some questions are followed by a line or a box. This shows you need to write a word, a few words or a sentence.

Marks

The number of marks in the margin tells you the maximum number of marks for each question.

You should work through the paper until you are asked to stop.

Work as quickly and as carefully as you can. If you finish before the end, go back and check your work.

You will have 45 minutes to answer the questions in this paper.

Grammar, Punctuation & Spelling

Test B, Paper 1: Questions

1. Underline the **verbs** in this sentence.

As the sun rose over the east coast it cast a pink glow over the land.

1

2. Add the correct **punctuation** to the end of this sentence.

These cases are very heavy, aren't they ☐

1

3. Draw lines to the correct labels for each sentence.

What a wet summer it has been	Question
This summer was the wettest on record	Exclamation
Stop raining now	Statement
Why has it been such a wet summer	Command

1

Marks

4. Draw lines to join the words to the correct **contraction**.

will not	willn't
	won't

should not	should'nt
	shouldn't

she has	she's
	shes'

what is	what's
	whats'

1

5. Underline the **main clause** in this sentence.

The houses were flooded again, even though there were flood defences.

1

6. Circle the best **synonym** to replace the underlined word. Circle **one**.

A <u>ferocious</u> tiger prowled around the edge of the trees.

hungry	vicious	terrifying

1

7. Rewrite this sentence in **Standard English**.

We was go to the park but it is rain.

_____

Marks

1

8. Use each **prefix** to make new words. Rewrite the new words in the space provided.

| in | ir | mis | de |

stabilise   _____

regular   _____

taken   _____

appropriately   _____

1

9. Draw a line to match each sentence with the best **punctuation**.

What an amazing sight
we saw

What is making you
look so amazed

What made us so amazed
were the fantastic fish

.

!

?

1

10. Change the underlined words to **plurals**.

The football <u>supporter</u> wore <u>a</u> black and amber <u>scarf</u>.

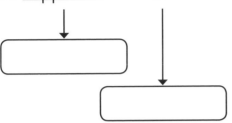

Marks

1

11. Underline the **pronouns** in these sentences.

She couldn't believe her parents' pleasure when they opened the present.

The children, who had been chosen, were practising hard.

1

12. Underline all the **adverbs**.

Since Shelley had arrived home early, she was able to unpack quickly before tea.

1

13. Find one more word for each **word family**.

extend   _____

double   _____

circle   _____

1

14. Rewrite this sentence in the **present progressive form**.

She spent all day wrapping birthday presents.

_____

1

15. Complete the sentences below using either **I** or **me**.

Why can't anyone see what _____ am looking at?

My dad helped my brother and _____ to tidy my
bedroom before tea.

1

16. This sentence has a **main clause** and an **adverbial** in it.

Singing softly, she picked up the baby.

a. Tick the **main clause**.

Tick **one**.

Singing softly	☐
she picked up	☐
she picked up the baby	☐

b. Tick the **adverbial**.

Tick **one**.

Singing softly	☐
she picked up	☐
she picked up the baby	☐

Marks

1

1

17. Choose the best word to go in each sentence.

Marks

| they're | their | there |

They had a lovely time unwrapping _____ presents.

Unfortunately _____ unable to attend the party.

_____ was a lot of birthday cake left over.

1

18. Match the beginning of the sentence to the correct ending.

are used to describe verbs.

join words, phrases and clauses.

Conjunctions

separate items in a list.

give additional information.

1

19. Underline the **subject** of this sentence.

The rain fell heavily all day.

1

20. Underline the **object** of this sentence.

Sunita saw a butterfly land nearby.

1

21. Insert three **apostrophes** in this sentence.

Theyre going to their caravan. Its a long way by car but that isnt a problem.

Marks

1

---

22. Tick all the **synonyms** for <u>determined</u>.

resolved ☐

resolute ☐

wavering ☐

firm ☐

1

---

23. Replace the underlined words with a **pronoun** in these sentences.

I cleaned <u>the fridge</u> out yesterday.

↓

[ ]

I invited <u>Abdul, Shamir and Emma</u> to my party.

↓

[ ]

1

Marks

24. Circle all the **determiners** in this sentence.

An old hag stumbled slowly towards the dark cave, which was surrounded by several vultures.

1

25. Put in the missing **commas** in this sentence.

The dog chewed my slippers the table leg a sock and even one of the toys!

1

26. In the sentence below, Mum made the pizza before putting it in the oven.

Complete the sentence with the correct **verb form**.

Although Mum _____ made the pizza, she still needed to put it in the oven to cook it.

1

27. Some of the **punctuation** is missing in the text below. Insert the correct punctuation into each of the boxes. Some boxes may need more than one punctuation mark.

☐ Look ☐ called Laura ☐ It's a beautiful sunset ☐

1

28. Which of the events below is **most** likely to happen?

Marks

Tick **one**.

We shall book a holiday later today. ☐

We can book a holiday later today. ☐

We will book a holiday later today. ☐

We may book a holiday later today. ☐

1

29. Circle the **relative clause** in the sentence below.

The red bike, which was very flashy, had been reduced.

1

30. Choose the correct **subordinating conjunction** to complete each sentence.

| if | because | although |

The children were worried _____ they could not do their homework in time.

I wanted to know _____ there was a train running on Sunday.

1

31. Underline the **prepositions** in the sentences below.

We bought tickets before the film.

We were all quite frightened during the film.

There was silence after the enthralling film.

Marks

1

32. Insert a **comma** and a **semi-colon** in the sentence below, to clarify its meaning.

Although only eight years old the girl's ability on the piano was outstanding she could play several classical pieces already.

1

33. The sentence below is written in the **active voice**.

Ellie read an interesting book about Spain.

Which sentence is written in the **passive form** of the sentence above?

Tick **one**.

An interesting book about Spain was read by Ellie. ☐

Ellie read an interesting book about Spain to me. ☐

The interesting book was about Spain. ☐

Reading the book about Spain was interesting. ☐

1

34. Tick one box in each row to show the **types of adverb**.

Marks

	Adverb of time	Adverb of possibility	Adverb of place
perhaps			
everywhere			
daily			

1

35. Choose the correct **relative pronoun** for each sentence.

who   whom

To _____ did James give his bag?

I often wondered _____ was responsible for that painting.

The police officer chased two burglars, one of _____ wore a mask.

1

36. Add these **suffixes** to the root words below to make **nouns**. You will need to use one suffix more than once.

You may need to take away or add other letters.

ance   ence   acy

private _____   lunatic _____

maintain _____   dependent _____

1

37. Tick one box in each row to show whether the word <u>after</u> is used as a **subordinating conjunction** or as a **preposition**.

Marks

Sentence	<u>after</u> used as a subordinating conjunction	<u>after</u> used as a preposition
We went for a pizza <u>after</u> the walk.		
I make my bed <u>after</u> I have had a wash.		
They needed to catch a bus <u>after</u> 3 o'clock in the afternoon.		

1

38. Which option completes the sentence below, so that it uses the **subjunctive mood**?

It would be really good if he _____ able to meet us after school.

Tick **one**.

were ☐

could be ☐

might be ☐

was ☐

1

SCHOLASTIC National Curriculum SATs Tests

Marks

39. Circle the word or words in the sentence below which make it a **question**.

This is a delicious cake, isn't it?

1

40. Tick **one** box to show the correct place to insert a **comma** in the sentence below.

Despite the early start they would not arrive until late.

1

41. Which of the sentences below uses **dashes** correctly?

Tick **one**.

The mountain was steep – almost vertical – so we had to climb slowly. ☐

The mountain was – steep almost vertical – so we had to climb slowly. ☐

The mountain – was steep almost vertical so – we had to climb slowly. ☐

The mountain was steep – almost vertical so – we had to climb slowly. ☐

1

42. a. Join the labels to the correct places in the text.

The birthday

paragraph 1

paragraph 2

heading

subheading

When my sister wanted to open her presents before her birthday, my mum told her she couldn't because she would have to wait. While my mum wasn't looking, my sister had a quick feel of them so she had a good idea what they were!

What a let down!

When her birthday came around, my sister felt very disappointed because she already knew what she was getting, so she wasn't surprised.

1

b. This text is split into two **paragraphs** because:

Tick **one**.

it is about two people. ☐

it was a let down. ☐

it is about before the girl's birthday and after her birthday. ☐

it is about being surprised and being disappointed. ☐

1

43. When my sister wanted to open her presents <u>before</u> her birthday

Circle **one**. In the phrase above the word <u>before</u> is used as:

an adverb	an adjective
a preposition	a determiner

Marks

1

44. <u>While</u> my mum wasn't looking,

The word <u>while</u> is used to introduce:

Tick **one**.

a noun phrase. ☐

a main clause. ☐

a subordinate clause. ☐

an adverbial phrase. ☐

1

45. Underline the **noun phrase** in the sentence below.

Every year our school has thirty new reception class pupils.

1

46. The phrase below would be clearer with a **hyphen**.

thirty new reception class pupils

Which of the phrases below uses a hyphen correctly?

Tick **one**.

thirty-new reception class pupils ☐

thirty new-reception class pupils ☐

thirty new reception-class pupils ☐

thirty new reception class-pupils ☐

1

47. Add three different **suffixes** to the word <u>child</u> to create new words. The first one has been done for you.

child**ish**

child_____

child_____

child_____

Marks

1

48. Circle two **determiners** in the sentence below.

Their parents look as worried as the children.

1

End of paper

Grammar, Punctuation & Spelling

Test B, Paper 2: Spelling

Instructions

- Your **spelling** will be tested in this paper.

- **20 short sentences** will be read aloud to you. A single word has been missed out of each sentence and you need to write this in the space provided.

- **You will hear each word three times.** The word will be said once, then read within a sentence, then repeated a third time. You should write the spelling in the space provided.

- All 20 sentences will be read again at the end, when you will be able to make any changes you wish to what you have written down.

- This paper should take approximately **15 minutes** to complete, although you will be allowed as much time as you need to complete the test.

1. There was a _____ noise coming from the ruined castle.

2. A _____ should include a subject and a verb.

3. The letter was _____ to the homeowner.

4. He had asked for a new _____ for his birthday.

5. The _____ of Queen Victoria lasted for over sixty years.

6. Judo is not an _____ sport.

7. We are learning to _____ different types of music.

8. Our school has an annual talent _____.

9. There is a _____ store in our village, which is open for long hours.

10. There was some _____ to the radio signal and we could not hear the programme.

Test B, Paper 2: Spelling

11. Our school _____ collects dinner money every Monday.

12. A girl from our school is hoping to become a _____ footballer.

13. The _____ for the concert snaked around the arena.

14. Their coach had _____ his free time to train them, but it had been worth it!

15. How long is the _____ on the laptop?

16. _____ calls often try to persuade us to buy or sign up for something.

17. I could go to the _____ centre to learn how to swim.

18. Although she tried to help with the cooking, it was more of a _____!

19. If you wish to open a savings account you will need two forms of _____.

20. My friends tried to _____ me to stay out longer.

End of paper

Question		Focus	Possible marks	Actual marks
Paper 1	1	Grammar: verbs	1	
	2	Punctuation: question marks	1	
	3	Grammar: sentence types	1	
	4	Punctuation: apostrophes for contraction	1	
	5	Grammar: clauses	1	
	6	Vocabulary: synonyms	1	
	7	Grammar: tenses	1	
	8	Vocabulary: prefixes	1	
	9	Punctuation: question marks, exclamation marks, full stops	1	
	10	Vocabulary: plurals	1	
	11	Grammar: pronouns	1	
	12	Grammar: adverbs	1	
	13	Vocabulary: word families	1	
	14	Grammar: verbs	1	
	15	Grammar: pronouns	1	
	16	Grammar: main clauses Grammar: fronted adverbials	2	
	17	Punctuation: apostrophes for contraction	1	
	18	Grammar: conjunctions	1	
	19	Grammar: subjects	1	
	20	Grammar: objects	1	
	21	Punctuation: apostrophes for contraction	1	
	22	Vocabulary: synonyms	1	
	23	Grammar: pronouns	1	
	24	Grammar: determiners	1	
	25	Punctuation: commas in lists	1	
	26	Grammar: verbs	1	
	27	Punctuation: speech	1	
	28	Grammar: modal verbs	1	
	29	Grammar: relative clauses	1	
	30	Grammar: subordinating conjunctions	1	
	31	Grammar: prepositions	1	
	32	Punctuation: commas, semi-colons	1	
	33	Grammar: passive voice	1	
	34	Grammar: adverbs	1	
	35	Grammar: relative pronouns	1	
	36	Vocabulary: suffixes	1	
	37	Grammar: subordinating conjunctions, prepositions	1	
	38	Grammar: subjunctive form	1	
	39	Grammar: question tags	1	
	40	Punctuation: commas after fronted adverbials	1	
	41	Punctuation: parenthesis	1	
	42	Grammar: paragraphs and headings	2	
	43	Grammar: word classes	1	
	44	Grammar: clauses	1	
	45	Grammar: noun phrases	1	
	46	Punctuation: hyphens	1	
	47	Vocabulary: suffixes	1	
	48	Grammar: determiners	1	
Paper 2	1–20	Spelling	20	
		Total	**70**	

Grammar, Punctuation & Spelling

Test C

Questions and answers

You have 45 minutes to complete this paper. There are different types of question for you to answer in different ways. The space for your answer shows you what type of answer is needed. Write your answer in the space provided.

- **Multiple choice answers:** for some questions you do not need to do any writing. Read the instructions carefully so you know how to answer the question.

- **Short answers:** some questions are followed by a line or a box. This shows you need to write a word, a few words or a sentence.

Marks

The number of marks in the margin tells you the maximum number of marks for each question.

You should work through the paper until you are asked to stop.

Work as quickly and as carefully as you can. If you finish before the end, go back and check your work.

You will have 45 minutes to answer the questions in this paper.

Test C, Paper 1: Questions

Marks

1. Underline the **adjectives** in this sentence.

The tall giraffes ravenously ate the thorny leaves of the bush.

1

2. Write an **exclamation** starting with *What*.

What _____

1

3. Choose a different **co-ordinating conjunction** to join the two parts of each sentence.

and   or   but

Would you like to go for a walk _____ ride your bike?

They needed to catch a bus _____ it was too late.

1

4. Tick the sentence which uses **capital letters** and **full stops** correctly.

Marks

Tick **one**.

Kylie and Ahmed wanted to go bowling they didn't have enough money. ☐

Kylie and Ahmed wanted to go bowling. they didn't have enough money ☐

Kylie and Ahmed wanted to go bowling. They didn't have enough money. ☐

Kylie and Ahmed wanted to go Bowling. They didn't have enough Money. ☐

1

5. Fill in the gaps below, using the **past progressive form** of the verbs in the box.

| to eat   to talk |

While I _____ my lunch, my friends

_____ loudly.

1

6. Circle each correct **contraction** in this sentence.

I **shouldnt'** / **shouldn't** go out when **it's** / **its'**

raining but **itl'l** / **it'll** be good fun.

1

7. Tick the sentence which is correctly **punctuated.**

Marks

Tick **one**.

"There's a full moon," tonight. said Josh. ☐

There's a "full moon, tonight." said Josh. ☐

"There's a full moon, tonight," said Josh. ☐

"There's a full moon, tonight said Josh." ☐

1

8. Insert the missing **apostrophes** in the correct places in these sentences.

Olivers pram wheels were so dirty that his parents couldnt remove the mud.

The three main banks interest rates were due to increase, much to their customers dissatisfaction.

1

Marks

9. Match the labels to the correct **sentence part**.

| main clause | subordinate clause |

The meal was ruined, despite the chef following the recipe.

1

10. Write a **relative clause** for this sentence.

The swimmer, _____, could see

a turtle.

1

11. Underline the **modal verb** in this sentence.

She might let him find it next week!

1

12. Replace the **object** in this sentence with a different one. Write your answer on the line below.

The angry dog jumped up at the door.

_____

1

13. Replace the **subject** in this sentence with a different one. Write your answer on the line below.

The boy drank from a tall, cool glass.

_____

Marks

1

14. Tick an **antonym** for prejudice.

Tick **one**.

bigotry ☐

unfairness ☐

tolerance ☐

discrimination ☐

1

15. Rewrite this sentence in the **present perfect tense**.

They learnt techniques for passing and dribbling the football.

_____

_____

1

16. Rewrite this sentence so that it is in the **past tense**.

They eat their tea and enjoy each other's company.

_____

_____

Marks

1

17. a. Choose the best **pronoun** to fit in the space in this sentence.

Although the weather was unusually cold, most

people were keeping warm and _____ hadn't caused a

major health risk.

Tick **one**.

my ☐

they ☐

we ☐

it ☐

1

b. <u>most</u> people were keeping warm
The word <u>most</u> is used as a:

Tick **one**.

determiner. ☐

possessive pronoun. ☐

preposition. ☐

pronoun. ☐

1

18. Rewrite this sentence, changing the **adverb**.

Liam walked slowly towards the football pitch.

_____

Marks

1

19. Join each sentence to its correct type.

Don't touch that broken glass!	Statement
What sharp glass that is!	Question
Do you want to cut yourself?	Exclamation
I can't believe you'd do that.	Command

1

20. Tick one box in each row to show how the **modal verb** affects the meaning of the sentence.

Sentence	Modal verb indicates certainty	Modal verb indicates possibility
They might arrive before dark.		
I can finish this homework tonight.		
We should tidy our bedrooms.		
He will bring the present with him.		

1

SCHOLASTIC National Curriculum SATs Tests

21. Harvey says, "Capital letters are only used at the beginning of a sentence." Is he correct?

Circle your answer.   Yes   No

Explain your reasons.

_____

_____

Marks

1

22. Draw lines to match each **prefix** with an ending to create a word.

anti		loyal
im		join
re		possible
dis		septic

1

23. Add **semi-colons** or **colons** to improve the clarity of these sentences.

School is to finish at 3.30pm ☐ this represents a change to our current timetable.

We visited Chatsworth, Haworth and Lyme Park in the north ☐ in the south we only saw Blenheim Palace and Oxford.

1

24. Rewrite the sentence below so it starts with an **adverbial**. Use the same words and remember to punctuate your answer.

We went on the swings after school.

_____

1

25. Match **two** sentences to each label.

The bright red car was stolen.

A thief stole the bright red car.

Passive voice

A baby bird was killed by the cat.

Active voice

The cat killed a baby bird.

1

26. Choose the best **adverb** to complete each sentence. Use each adverb **once**.

next   therefore   soon

_____ it became clear that snow had blocked the road.

Let's see who arrives _____.

The meeting has been cancelled; we shall _____ need to arrange a future meeting.

1

Marks

27. <u>The glistening white snow</u> crunched under their feet. Circle **one**.

The words <u>the glistening white snow</u> are:

an adjective	a noun
an adverbial	a noun phrase

1

28. Tick **one** box in this sentence to show the correct place to use a **semi-colon**.

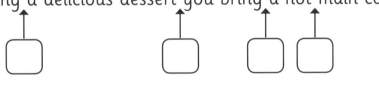

I will bring a delicious dessert you bring a hot main course.

1

29. Tick one box in each row to show if each sentence uses **formal** or **informal vocabulary**.

Sentence	Formal	Informal
I am asking if the job is still free.		
I am enquiring if the position is still vacant.		
I requested a rise in my salary.		
I wanted to be paid more money.		

1

30. Choose a **suffix** to change these words into **adjectives**. Rewrite the new words in full in the space provided. You may need to change some letters.

Marks

less	ness	ment	ful

penny   _____

plenty   _____

worth   _____

1

31. Choose a **suffix** to change these words into **nouns**. Rewrite the new words in full in the space provided. You may need to change some letters.

tion	ness	ment

cheerful   _____

define   _____

embarrass   _____

1

32. Explain how the use of a **hyphen** changes the meaning in these sentences.

We were impressed by the <u>changing room.</u>

We were impressed by the <u>changing-room.</u>

_____

_____

1

33. Tick the sentence that uses a **single dash** correctly.

Marks

Tick **one**.

Some writers – still like to use pens and paper, I prefer my tablet. ☐

Some writers still like to use pens and paper – I prefer my tablet. ☐

Some writers still like to use pens – and paper, I prefer my tablet. ☐

Some writers still like to use pens and paper, I prefer – my tablet. ☐

1

34. Tick the sentence that uses commas correctly to show **parenthesis**.

Tick **one**.

My brother who missed, the bus, was late for school. ☐

My brother, who missed the bus was late, for school. ☐

My brother, who missed the bus, was late for school. ☐

My brother who, missed the bus was late for, school. ☐

1

35. Which option completes the sentence below so that it uses the **subjunctive mood**?

Marks

It is very important that everyone who is in the school play _____ at the final rehearsal.

Tick **one**.

is at ☐

will be ☐

be ☐

are ☐

1

36. Rewrite this list, using a **colon** and **bullet points**.

I need to buy some oranges, apples and a piece of string.

_____

_____

_____

1

SCHOLASTIC National Curriculum SATs Tests

37. Underline the word which does not belong to each **word family**.

commute	communication	communicates	communicative
exaggerates	excellence	exaggeration	exaggerating
disinterested	uninteresting	identification	interests
insincere	sincerely	sincerest	sufficiently

Marks

1

38. Use a different **conjunction** to complete these sentences.

while   after   so

I chose an ice cream _____ I had eaten my main course.

I used my umbrella _____ the rain was falling.

I ran _____ I could catch the bus.

1

39. Which sentence is written in the **active voice**?

Tick **one**.

The car was brought into the garage for servicing. ☐

The garage was very busy with cars needing repair. ☐

The problem was caused by the age of the cars. ☐

Some expensive bills were received by the owners. ☐

1

40. Change the **noun phrase** in this sentence to one with an opposite meaning. Rewrite the noun phrase below.

It was a clear bright day and they were enjoying the walk.

_____

1

41. Tick one box in each row to show the **function** of each part of the sentence below.

During the evening, there was lots of food and we even played some games.

	Clause	Adverbial	Co-ordinating conjunction
During the evening,			
there was lots of food			
and			
we even played some games			

1

42. Write the correct term for each **layout device** in the boxes.

Marks

TESTS ←[   ]   [   ]
                                          ↓

All Year 6 pupils in England take the **Key Stage 2 tests**.
Here are some ways to prepare for them:

- Revise thoroughly. ←[   ]
- Use practice tests.

1

43. Change these words by adding or subtracting a **suffix**.

Adverb	thoroughly	**Verb**	prepare
Noun	_____	**Noun**	_____

1

44. Add a **prefix** to change the word <u>prepared</u> into its **antonym**.

_____prepared

1

45. To make bread you need:

- flour • yeast • salt • sugar • oil • water

In the above clause, the **colon** is used to:

Tick **one**.

separate items in a list. ☐

introduce an important point. ☐

introduce a list. ☐

separate clauses. ☐

1

46. Join each sentence or clause to its **tense**.

Marks

Sentence	Tense
My dad has looked for the television control.	Present progressive
She had hidden it.	Present perfect
My mum is smiling.	Past perfect

1

47. Tick the **past progressive form** of <u>My mum is smiling.</u>

Tick **one**.

My mum smiled. ☐

My mum has smiled. ☐

My mum was smiling. ☐

My mum had smiled. ☐

1

Marks

48. He always switches over to football <u>when</u> she is watching something she likes.

The word <u>when</u> in the above text is used as a:

Tick one.

co-ordinating conjunction. ☐

subordinating conjunction. ☐

preposition of time. ☐

preposition of place. ☐

1

49. My dad has looked for the television control for the last week.

Tick one box in each row to show the **function** of each part of this sentence.

Sentence	Adverbial	Subject	Object	Verb
My dad				
has looked				
the television control				
for the last week				

1

End of paper

Grammar, Punctuation & Spelling

Test C, Paper 2: Spelling

Instructions

- Your **spelling** will be tested in this paper.

- **20 short sentences** will be read aloud to you. A single word has been missed out of each sentence and you need to write this in the space provided.

- **You will hear each word three times.** The word will be said once, then read within a sentence, then repeated a third time. You should write the spelling in the space provided.

- All 20 sentences will be read again at the end, when you will be able to make any changes you wish to what you have written down.

- This paper should take approximately **15 minutes** to complete, although you will be allowed as much time as you need to complete the test.

SCHOLASTIC National Curriculum SATs Tests

1. The new _____ was developing very quickly.

2. His parents were waiting for his flight's _____.

3. _____ we will be able to read the book again tomorrow.

4. A hexagon has six _____ sides.

5. The _____ was quite tricky but she managed to complete it.

6. She had been an _____ gymnast for a few years.

7. Ben opened the _____ to the email, wondering what was inside it.

8. She became _____ of lots of people looking at her.

9. I will _____ see you tomorrow.

10. It was a fantastic _____ and he wouldn't turn it down.

11. Some people believe in the _____ of the

Loch Ness monster.

12. There was a lot of _____ when they arrived on

the wrong day.

13. They couldn't work out what _____ the children

were speaking.

14. He had _____ ache all morning.

15. The secretary had a lot of _____ to deal with.

16. The doctor gave him a _____ examination.

17. He joined the army to become a _____.

18. There is a wide choice of _____ for school leavers.

19. The _____ of consonants is very different in Spanish.

20. We are _____ proud to announce the winner of

the courtesy award.

End of paper

Question		Focus	Possible marks	Actual marks
Paper 1	1	Grammar: adjectives	1	
	2	Grammar: exclamations	1	
	3	Grammar: co-ordinating conjunctions	1	
	4	Punctuation: capital letters and full stops	1	
	5	Grammar: tenses	1	
	6	Punctuation: apostrophes for contraction	1	
	7	Punctuation: inverted commas	1	
	8	Punctuation: apostrophes for possession	1	
	9	Grammar: main clauses and subordinate clauses	1	
	10	Grammar: relative clauses	1	
	11	Grammar: modal verbs	1	
	12	Grammar: objects	1	
	13	Grammar: subjects	1	
	14	Vocabulary: antonyms	1	
	15	Grammar: tenses	1	
	16	Grammar: tenses	1	
	17	Grammar: pronouns	2	
	18	Grammar: adverbs	1	
	19	Grammar: sentence types	1	
	20	Grammar: modal verbs	1	
	21	Grammar: capital letters	1	
	22	Vocabulary: prefixes	1	
	23	Punctuation: colons and semi-colons	1	
	24	Grammar: fronted adverbials	1	
	25	Grammar: active voice and passive voice	1	
	26	Grammar: adverbs of time, place and cause	1	
	27	Grammar: noun phrases	1	
	28	Punctuation: semi-colons	1	
	29	Grammar: formal and informal	1	
	30	Vocabulary: suffixes	1	
	31	Vocabulary: suffixes	1	
	32	Punctuation: hyphens	1	
	33	Punctuation: single dashes	1	
	34	Punctuation: parenthesis	1	
	35	Grammar: subjunctive	1	
	36	Punctuation: colons and bullet-pointed lists	1	
	37	Vocabulary: word families	1	
	38	Grammar: conjunctions	1	
	39	Grammar: active voice	1	
	40	Grammar: noun phrases	1	
	41	Grammar: clauses, adverbials and conjunctions	1	
	42	Grammar: headings and layout	1	
	43	Vocabulary: suffixes	1	
	44	Vocabulary: prefixes	1	
	45	Punctuation: colons	1	
	46	Grammar: tenses	1	
	47	Grammar: verbs	1	
	48	Grammar: subordinating conjunctions	1	
	49	Grammar: word classes	1	
Paper 2	1–20	Spelling	20	
		Total	**70**	

Marks & guidance

Marking and assessing the papers

Grammar, punctuation, vocabulary and spelling, where appropriate in the tests, have right/wrong answers. However, there are some open-ended questions that require the children's input. For these questions, example answers have been provided. However, they are not exhaustive and alternatives are appropriate, so careful marking and a certain degree of interpretation will be needed.

Marking paper 1: questions

Question type	Accept	Do not accept
Tick boxes	Clear unambiguous marks.	Responses where more boxes have been ticked than required.
Circling or underlining	Clear unambiguous indication of the correct answer – including a box.	Responses where more than the required number of words have been circled or underlined. Responses where the correct answer is circled or underlined, together with surrounding words. Answers in which less than half of the required word is circled or underlined.
Drawing lines	Lines that do not touch the boxes, provided the intention is clear.	Multiple lines drawn to or from the same box (unless a requirement of the question).
Labelling parts of speech	Clear labels, whether they use the full vocabulary required by the question or an unambiguous abbreviation.	Ambiguity in labelling such as the use of 'CN' when asked to identify collective nouns and common nouns.
Punctuation	Punctuation that is clear, unambiguous and recognisable as the required punctuation mark.	Punctuation that is ambiguous, for example if it is unclear whether the mark is a comma or full stop.
Spelling	Where no specific mark scheme guidance is given, incorrect spellings of the correct response should be accepted.	Correct spelling is generally required for questions assessing contracted forms, plurals, verb tenses, prefixes and suffixes.

Marking paper 2: spelling

- If more than one attempt is made, it must be clear which version the child wishes to be marked.

- Spellings can be written in upper or lower case, or a mixture of the two.

- If a word has been written with the correct sequence of letters but they have been separated into clearly divided components, with or without a dash, the mark is not awarded.

- If a word has been written with the correct sequence of letters but an apostrophe or hyphen has been inserted, the mark is not awarded.

- Any acceptable British-English spelling can be marked as correct. For example, *organise* or *organize*.

Marks table

At the end of each test there is a table for you to insert the number of marks achieved for each question. This will enable you to see which areas your child needs to practise further.

National standard in Grammar, Punctuation & Spelling

The mark that the child gets in the test paper will be known as the 'raw score' (for example, '38' in 38/70). The raw score will be converted to a scaled score and children achieving a scaled score of 100 or more will achieve the national standard in that subject. These 'scaled scores' enable results to be reported consistently year-on-year.

The guidance in the table below shows the marks that children need to achieve to reach the national standard. This should be treated as a guide only as the number of marks may vary. You can also find up-to-date information about scaled scores on our website: www.scholastic.co.uk/nationaltests

Marks achieved	Standard
0–37	Has not met the national standard in Grammar, Punctuation & Spelling for KS2
38–70	Has met the national standard in Grammar, Punctuation & Spelling for KS2

Q	Answers	Marks
1	It is a sunny day**.** What a sunny day**!** When is it going to be sunny**?**	1
2	<u>The</u> dragon went to <u>a</u> cave and blew out <u>some</u> enormous flames.	1
3	The frost glistened like <u>chilly</u>, <u>white</u> icing. The sea lapped lazily onto the <u>soft</u>, <u>golden</u> sand.	1
4	(princess)(elizabeth) married her husband, (philip) of (greece), in (november) 1947 in (london).	1
5	"Look at all that mud!" exclaimed Mum. "You really need to dry the dog when you bring her in."	1
6	<u>Your dad and I</u> will increase your pocket money next month. ↓ [we] My pencil's gone. May I borrow <u>your pencil</u>? ↓ [yours]	1
7	Despite eating a healthy diet, <u>many people still suffer from heart disease</u>.	1
8	mine	1
9	You have arrived early, haven't you	1
10	Our village has held a summer fete this year.	1
11	You must learn these spellings by next week.	1
12	are were	1
13	,	1
14	careful**ly** quick**ly** mysterious**ly** happi**ly**	1
15	can't wouldn't I'll we're	1
16	**Accept** any adjective which is an antonym of grotesque. For example: beautiful/lovely/attractive	1
17	**dis**respect **in**appropriate **re**produce **un**attractive	1
18	Amy and Jack **go** to the cinema each Monday.	1
19	**a.** The harvest basket was full of apples, oranges, pears and bananas.	1
	b. To separate items in a list.	1

Q	Answers	Marks
20	even though	1
21	They had a wonderful holiday **because** the weather was hot and sunny. Ahmed and Sunita will be very cold **if** they do not wear their coats.	1
22	New Year is celebrated (after) Christmas. The match was abandoned (because of) the fog. The explorers discovered North America (during) the fifteenth century.	1
23	They were thrilled by the two boys' diving display. The team's goal caused an uproar.	1
24	Near the reef, there was a great variety of marine life, manta rays, stingrays, turtles and even baby sharks! [:]	1
25	We went to the park to meet our friends. **Accept** any subordinate clause which makes sense. For example: to play on the swings. End punctuation (. !?) must be included.	1
26	They will go to the cinema this evening.	1
27	that	1
28	round	1
29	[✓] The flight was very long and arduous it was a relief when we landed.	1
30	It uses commas to clarify meaning. It uses adverbials to order the text. It is written in the present tense.	1
31	[it] → [budget]	1
32	an adverbial phrase.	1
33	Everything happened so quickly: a swirl of brown, a whirl of white and the sausages flew out of sight! Who could have done it? **Accept** semi-colon/dash instead of colon.	1
34	They asked her, "Do you want to/Would you like to come to the party?"	1
35	<table><tr><td>Sentence</td><td>Adverb of time</td><td>Adverb of place</td><td>Adverb of possibility</td></tr></table>	1

Q35 table:

Sentence	Adverb of time	Adverb of place	Adverb of possibility
We were soon able to reach the summit.	✓		
They would surely reach the summit before night.			✓
If they kept moving forwards they would reach the summit.		✓	

■SCHOLASTIC National Curriculum SATs Tests

Q	Answers	Marks
36	**a.** brackets	I
	b. It is used to separate additional information.	I
37	Jack, (who) was very hungry, went home for tea. The goal, (which) the opposing team scored, was an own goal.	I
38	decrease → increase valuable → worthless malicious → kind abundant → scarce	I
39	I wish I were on holiday.	I
40	**a.** don't they?	I
	b. To encourage the reader/listener to agree with the writer/speaker.	I
41	**formal:** You cannot have anything. Would you please pass me the cake.	I
	informal: I ain't giving you any. Gimme the cake.	
42	The performance includes: a famous folk singer, the local brass band, an enthralling magician and a cheeky ventriloquist.	I
43	**a. Accept** any answer that uses 'judge' as a noun, for example: *The judge gave a guilty verdict.*	I
	b. Accept any answer that uses 'judge' as a verb, for example: *They were learning to judge the mass of different objects.*	I

44	Active voice	Passive voice	Marks
	The bird ate the nuts.	The nuts were eaten by the bird.	I
	Jamal read his book.	**The/His book was read by Jamal.**	
	The theatre put on a great show.	**A great show was put on by the theatre.**	

45	Word	Pronoun	Adjective	Verb	Preposition	Noun	Marks
	overdue		✓				2
	it	✓					
	steam					✓	
	rose			✓			
	under				✓		

2 marks: all correct
I mark: 3–4 correct

	Total	**50**

Test A, Paper 2: Spelling test script and mark scheme

This spelling test can be found on pages 28–30.

Notes for conducting the spelling test

The paper should take approximately **15 minutes** to complete, although you should allow children as much time as they need to complete it.

Read the instructions below to the children.

> *Listen carefully to the instructions I am going to give you.*
>
> *I am going to read 20 sentences to you. Each sentence has a word missing. You should listen carefully to the missing word and fill this in, making sure you spell it correctly.*
>
> *I will read the word, then the word within a sentence, then repeat the word a third time.*
>
> *Do you have any questions?*
>
> Then read the spellings to the children as follows:
>
> **1.** Give the spelling number.
>
> **2.** Say 'The word is...'.
>
> **3.** Read the context sentence.
>
> **4.** Repeat 'The word is...'.
>
> Leave at least a 12-second gap between spellings.
>
> At the end, re-read all 20 questions. Then say *This is the end of the test please put down your pen or pencil.*

Each correct answer should be awarded **1 mark**. For more information on marking this paper, please refer to page 82.

Spelling one: the word is **disliked**.

Amy **disliked** watching football on television.

The word is **disliked**.

Spelling two: the word is **curiosity**.

His **curiosity** got the better of him and he began to open the parcel.

The word is **curiosity**.

Spelling three: the word is **clapping**.

The audience was **clapping** for a long time after the final bow.

The word is **clapping**.

Spelling four: the word is **caught**.

Ellie **caught** chickenpox from one of her friends.

The word is **caught**.

Spelling five: the word is **necessary**.

We need to ensure we pack all the **necessary** medications.

The word is **necessary**.

Spelling six: the word is **replied**.

Oscar **replied** enthusiastically to the teacher's question.

The word is **replied**.

Spelling seven: the word is **character**.

Most novels have a good and a bad **character**.

The word is **character**.

Spelling eight: the word is **autobiography**.

Many famous people write an **autobiography** which goes on sale just before Christmas.

The word is **autobiography**.

Spelling nine: the word is **programme**.

Sometimes, it can be difficult to know which **programme** to watch on television.

The word is **programme**.

Spelling ten: the word is **irregular**.

An **irregular** polygon does not have equal sides or angles.

The word is **irregular**.

Spelling eleven: the word is **although**.

Rashid missed the bus **although** he might have caught it if he had left earlier.

The word is **although**.

Spelling twelve: the word is **imagination**.

Use your **imagination** to help you create an exciting adventure.

The word is **imagination**.

Spelling thirteen: the word is **ceiling**.

Painting the **ceiling** was a long and difficult job.

The word is **ceiling**.

Spelling fourteen: the word is **remembrance**.

There are **remembrance** ceremonies on 11 November every year.

The word is **remembrance**.

Spelling fifteen: the word is **temperature**.

The **temperature** on Friday was below zero.

The word is **temperature**.

Spelling sixteen: the word is **neighbours**.

Our **neighbours** are very friendly.

The word is **neighbours**.

Spelling seventeen: the word is **bruise**.

After a collision in netball, Jamilla received a large **bruise**.

The word is **bruise**.

Spelling eighteen: the word is **dictionary**.

Use a **dictionary** to help you spell tricky words.

The word is **dictionary**.

Spelling nineteen: the word is **forty**.

My dad was **forty** on Monday.

The word is **forty**.

Spelling twenty: the word is **frequently**.

We **frequently** go to see my grandparents.

The word is **frequently**.

Q	Answers	Marks
1	As the sun <u>rose</u> over the east coast it <u>cast</u> a pink glow over the land.	1
2	These cases are very heavy, aren't they**?**	1

3

		Marks
What a wet summer it has been	Question	1
This summer was the wettest on record	Exclamation	
Stop raining now	Statement	
Why has it been such a wet summer	Command	

What a wet summer it has been → Exclamation
This summer was the wettest on record → Statement
Stop raining now → Command
Why has it been such a wet summer → Question

4

will not → won't
she has → she's
should not → shouldn't
what is → what's

Mark: 1

5	<u>The houses were flooded again</u>, even though there were flood defences.	1
6	vicious	1
7	We **were going** to the park but it **was raining**.	1
8	**de**stabilise **ir**regular **mis**taken **in**appropriately	1

9

Sentence	Punctuation	Marks
What an amazing sight we saw	.	1
What is making you look so amazed	!	
What made us so amazed were the fantastic fish	?	

What an amazing sight we saw → !
What is making you look so amazed → ?
What made us so amazed were the fantastic fish → .

Q	Answers	Marks
10	The football <u>supporter</u> wore <u>a</u> black and amber <u>scarf</u>. supporter → **supporters** a → **some** scarf → **scarves** **Also accept** any suitable plural determiner to replace 'a'. For example: several/many/two.	I
11	<u>She</u> couldn't believe <u>her</u> parents' pleasure when <u>they</u> opened the present. The children, <u>who</u> had been chosen, were practising hard.	I
12	<u>Since</u> Shelley had arrived home <u>early</u>, she was able to unpack <u>quickly</u> before tea.	I
13	extend: extension, extensive double: doubled, doubling circle: circular, circling **Accept** any word which belongs to above word families.	I
14	She **is spending** all day wrapping birthday presents.	I
15	Why can't anyone see what **I** am looking at? My dad helped my brother and **me** to tidy my bedroom before tea.	I
16	**a.** she picked up the baby	I
	b. Singing softly	I
17	They had a lovely time unwrapping **their** presents. Unfortunately **they're** unable to attend the party. **There** was a lot of birthday cake left over.	I
18	Conjunctions → join words, phrases and clauses.	I
19	<u>The rain</u> fell heavily all day.	I
20	Sunita saw <u>a butterfly</u> land nearby.	I
21	They're going to their caravan. It's a long way by car but that isn't a problem.	I
22	resolved resolute firm	I
23	I cleaned <u>the fridge</u> out yesterday. the fridge → **it** I invited <u>Abdul, Shamir and Emma</u> to my party. Abdul, Shamir and Emma → **them**	I

SCHOLASTIC National Curriculum SATs Tests

Q	Answers	Marks
24	(An) old hag stumbled slowly towards (the) dark cave, which was surrounded by (several) vultures.	1
25	The dog chewed my slippers, the table leg, a sock and even one of the toys!	1
26	Although Mum **had** made the pizza, she still needed to put it in the oven to cook it.	1
27	"Look!/," called Laura. "It's a beautiful sunset."	1
28	We will book a holiday later today.	1
29	The red bike, (which was very flashy,) had been reduced.	1
30	The children were worried **because** they could not do their homework in time. I wanted to know **if** there was a train running on Sunday.	1
31	We bought tickets <u>before</u> the film. We were all quite frightened <u>during</u> the film. There was silence <u>after</u> the enthralling film.	1
32	Although only eight years old, the girl's ability on the piano was outstanding; she could play several classical pieces already.	1
33	An interesting book about Spain was read by Ellie.	1

34

	Adverb of time	Adverb of possibility	Adverb of place
perhaps		✓	
everywhere			✓
daily	✓		

(Marks: 1)

Q	Answers	Marks
35	To **whom** did James give his bag? I often wondered **who** was responsible for that painting. The police officer chased two burglars, one of **whom** wore a mask.	1
36	priv**acy** mainten**ance** lun**acy** depend**ence**	1

Q	Answers	Marks

37

Sentence	**after** used as a subordinating conjunction	**after** used as a preposition
We went for a pizza <u>after</u> the walk.		✓
I make my bed <u>after</u> I have had a wash.	✓	
They needed to catch a bus <u>after</u> 3 o'clock in the afternoon.		✓

Marks: I

38 were — I

39 This is a delicious cake, (isn't it)?

Also accept responses which circle the comma and/or the question mark in addition to the correct words. — I

40 Despite the early start they would not arrive until late.

— I

41 The mountain was steep – almost vertical – so we had to climb slowly. — I

42 **a.**

The birthday

paragraph 1

paragraph 2

heading

subheading

When my sister wanted to open her presents before her birthday, my mum told her she couldn't because she would have to wait. While my mum wasn't looking, my sister had a quick feel of them so she had a good idea what they were!

What a let down!

When her birthday came around, my sister felt very disappointed because she already knew what she was getting, so she wasn't surprised.

Marks: I

b. it is about before the girl's birthday and after her birthday. — I

43 a preposition — I

44 a subordinate clause. — I

45 Every year our school has <u>thirty new reception class pupils</u>. — I

46 thirty new reception-class pupils — I

47 child<u>hood</u>; child<u>like</u>; child<u>less</u>. Also accept child<u>ishly</u> and child<u>ren</u>. — I

48 (Their) parents look as worried as (the) children. — I

	Total	**50**

SCHOLASTIC National Curriculum SATs Tests

This spelling test can be found on pages 52–54.

Notes for conducting the spelling test

The paper should take approximately **15 minutes** to complete, although you should allow children as much time as they need to complete it.

Read the instructions below to the children.

Listen carefully to the instructions I am going to give you.

I am going to read 20 sentences to you. Each sentence has a word missing. You should listen carefully to the missing word and fill this in, making sure you spell it correctly.

I will read the word, then the word within a sentence, then repeat the word a third time.

Do you have any questions?

Then read the spellings to the children as follows:

1. Give the spelling number.

2. Say 'The word is...'.

3. Read the context sentence.

4. Repeat 'The word is...'.

Leave at least a 12-second gap between spellings.

At the end, re-read all 20 questions. Then say *This is the end of the test please put down your pen or pencil.*

Each correct answer should be awarded **1 mark**. For more information on marking this paper, please refer to page 82.

Spelling one: the word is **strange**.

There was a **strange** noise coming from the ruined castle.

The word is **strange**.

Spelling two: the word is **sentence**.

A **sentence** should include a subject and a verb.

The word is **sentence**.

Spelling three: the word is **addressed**.

The letter was **addressed** to the homeowner.

The word is **addressed**.

Spelling four: the word is **bicycle**.

He had asked for a new **bicycle** for his birthday.

The word is **bicycle**.

Spelling five: the word is **reign**.

The **reign** of Queen Victoria lasted for over sixty years.

The word is **reign**.

Spelling six: the word is **aggressive**.

Judo is not an **aggressive** sport.

The word is **aggressive**.

Spelling seven: the word is **appreciate**.

We are learning to **appreciate** different types of music.

The word is **appreciate**.

Spelling eight: the word is **competition**.

Our school has an annual talent **competition**.

The word is **competition**.

Spelling nine: the word is **convenience**.

There is a **convenience** store in our village, which is open for long hours.

The word is **convenience**.

Spelling ten: the word is **interference**.

There was some **interference** to the radio signal and we could not hear the programme.

The word is **interference**.

Spelling eleven: the word is **secretary**.

Our school **secretary** collects dinner money every Monday.

The word is **secretary**.

Spelling twelve: the word is **professional**.

A girl from our school is hoping to become a **professional** footballer.

The word is **professional**.

Spelling thirteen: the word is **queue**.

The **queue** for the concert snaked around the arena.

The word is **queue**.

Spelling fourteen: the word is **sacrificed**.

Their coach had **sacrificed** his free time to train them, but it had been worth it!

The word is **sacrificed**.

Spelling fifteen: the word is **guarantee**.

How long is the **guarantee** on the laptop?

The word is **guarantee**.

Spelling sixteen: the word is **nuisance**.

Nuisance calls often try to persuade us to buy or sign up for something.

The word is **nuisance**.

Spelling seventeen: the word is **leisure**.

I could go to the **leisure** centre to learn how to swim.

The word is **leisure**.

Spelling eighteen: the word is **hindrance**.

Although she tried to help with the cooking, it was more of a **hindrance**!

The word is **hindrance**.

Spelling nineteen: the word is **identification**.

If you wish to open a savings account you will need two forms of **identification**.

The word is **identification**.

Spelling twenty: the word is **persuade**.

My friends tried to **persuade** me to stay out longer.

The word is **persuade**.

Q	Answers	Marks
1	The <u>tall</u> giraffes ravenously ate the <u>thorny</u> leaves of the bush.	1
2	**Accept** any appropriate exclamation which ends with an exclamation mark. For example: What a beautiful baby you have!	1
3	Would you like to go for a walk **or** ride your bike? They needed to catch a bus **but** it was too late.	1
4	Kylie and Ahmed wanted to go bowling. They didn't have enough money.	1
5	While I **was eating** my lunch, my friends **were talking** loudly.	1
6	I shouldnt' /(shouldn't) go out when (it's)/ its' raining but itl'l /(it'll) be good fun.	1
7	"There's a full moon tonight," said Josh.	1
8	Oliver**'**s pram wheels were so dirty that his parents couldn**'**t remove the mud. The three main banks**'** interest rates were due to increase, much to their customers**'** dissatisfaction.	1
9	main clause subordinate clause ↓ ↓ The meal was ruined, despite the chef following the recipe.	1
10	**Accept** any appropriate relative clause. For example: The swimmer, **who was snorkelling**, could see a turtle.	1
11	She <u>might</u> let him find it next week.	1
12	**Accept** any appropriate noun. For example: The angry dog jumped up at **the gate**.	1
13	**Accept** any appropriate noun. For example: The **woman** drank from a tall, cool glass. **Also accept** names of people. For example: Megan.	1
14	tolerance	1
15	They **have** learnt techniques for passing and dribbling the football.	1
16	They **ate** their tea and **enjoyed** each other's company.	1
17	**a.** it **b.** determiner.	1 1
18	**Accept** any appropriate adverb. For example: Liam walked **quickly** towards the football pitch.	1

Q	Answers	Marks

19

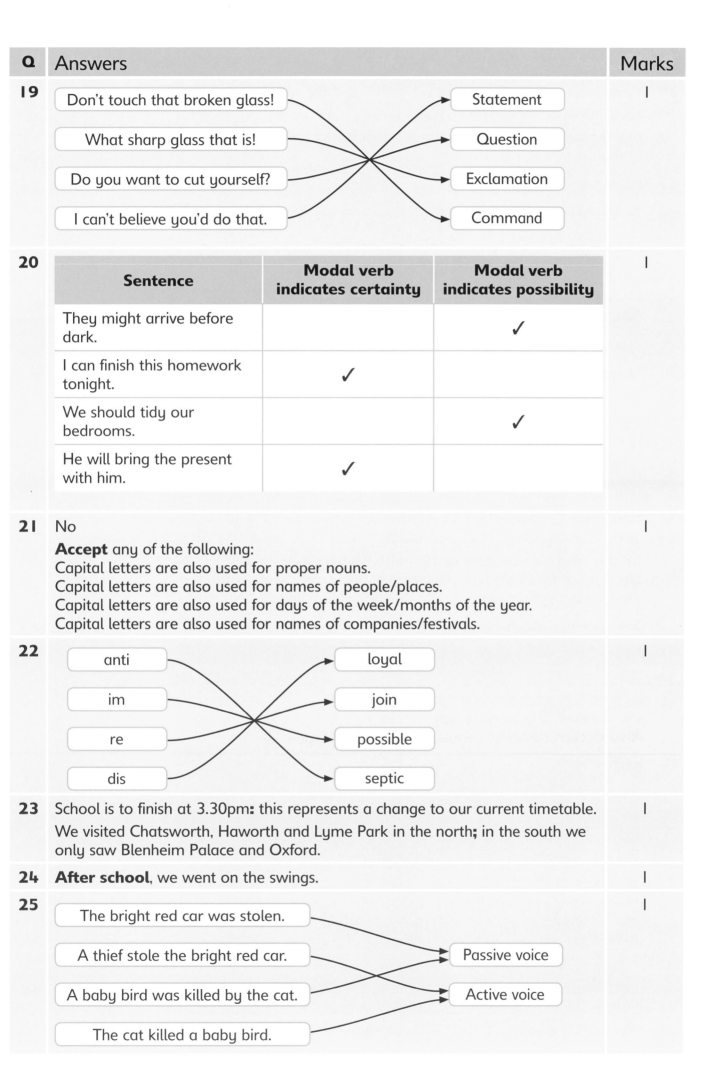

Don't touch that broken glass! → Command

What sharp glass that is! → Exclamation

Do you want to cut yourself? → Question

I can't believe you'd do that. → Statement

Marks: I

20

Sentence	Modal verb indicates certainty	Modal verb indicates possibility
They might arrive before dark.		✓
I can finish this homework tonight.	✓	
We should tidy our bedrooms.		✓
He will bring the present with him.	✓	

Marks: I

21 No

Accept any of the following:
Capital letters are also used for proper nouns.
Capital letters are also used for names of people/places.
Capital letters are also used for days of the week/months of the year.
Capital letters are also used for names of companies/festivals.

Marks: I

22

anti → septic

im → possible

re → join

dis → loyal

Marks: I

23 School is to finish at 3.30pm: this represents a change to our current timetable.

We visited Chatsworth, Haworth and Lyme Park in the north; in the south we only saw Blenheim Palace and Oxford.

Marks: I

24 **After school**, we went on the swings.

Marks: I

25

The bright red car was stolen. → Passive voice

A thief stole the bright red car. → Active voice

A baby bird was killed by the cat. → Passive voice

The cat killed a baby bird. → Active voice

Marks: I

Q	Answers	Marks
26	**Soon** it became clear that snow had blocked the road. Let's see who arrives **next**. The meeting has been cancelled; we shall **therefore** need to arrange a future meeting.	I
27	a noun phrase	I
28	I will bring a delicious dessert you bring a hot main course. ↑ ☑	I

29

Sentence	Formal	Informal
I am asking if the job is still free.		✓
I am enquiring if the position is still vacant.	✓	
I requested a rise in my salary.	✓	
I wanted to be paid more money.		✓

Marks: I

Q	Answers	Marks
30	penn**iless**, plent**iful**, worth**less**	I
31	cheerful**ness**, defini**tion**, embarrass**ment**	I
32	**Award I mark** for responses that indicate that in sentence I the room may be changing (into something different); whereas in sentence 2 it is a room for changing clothes (for example after swimming/gym). **Do not accept** responses that only explain the meaning of one sentence.	I
33	Some writers still like to use pens and paper – I prefer my tablet.	I
34	My brother, who missed the bus, was late for school.	I
35	be	I
36	I need to buy: • some oranges • apples • a piece of string. **Also accept** capitalisation of all three ingredients. **Also accept** consistent use of commas or semi-colons at the end of the first two items with a full stop after the third. **Do not accept** inconsistency in punctuation or capitalisation.	I
37	commute excellence identification sufficiently	I
38	I chose an ice cream **after** I had eaten my main course. I used my umbrella **while** the rain was falling. I ran **so** I could catch the bus.	I
39	The garage was very busy with cars needing repair.	I

SCHOLASTIC National Curriculum SATs Tests

Q	Answers	Marks
40	**Accept** any sensible replacement which has an opposite meaning. For example: cloudy dark night/cloudy dark day.	I

41

	Clause	Adverbial	Co-ordinating conjunction
During the evening,		✓	
there was lots of food	✓		
and			✓
we even played some games	✓		

Marks: I

42

TESTS ← [Heading]   [Bold text]

All Year 6 pupils in England take the **Key Stage 2 tests**. Here are some ways to prepare for them:
- Revise thoroughly. ← [Bullet points]
- Use practice tests.

Marks: I

Q	Answers	Marks
43	thoroughness preparation/preparations	I
44	**un**prepared	I
45	introduce a list.	I

46

Sentence	Tense
My dad has looked for the television control.	Present progressive
She had hidden it.	Present perfect
My mum is smiling.	Past perfect

(My dad has looked → Present perfect; She had hidden it → Past perfect; My mum is smiling → Present progressive)

Marks: I

Q	Answers	Marks
47	My mum was smiling.	I
48	subordinating conjunction.	I

49

Sentence	Adverbial	Subject	Object	Verb
My dad		✓		
has looked				✓
the television control			✓	
for the last week	✓			

Marks: I

Total: 50

Test C, Paper 2: Spelling test script and mark scheme

This spelling test can be found on pages 76–78.

Notes for conducting the spelling test

The paper should take approximately **15 minutes** to complete, although you should allow children as much time as they need to complete it.

Read the instructions below to the children.

Listen carefully to the instructions I am going to give you.

I am going to read 20 sentences to you. Each sentence has a word missing. You should listen carefully to the missing word and fill this in, making sure you spell it correctly.

I will read the word, then the word within a sentence, then repeat the word a third time.

Do you have any questions?

Then read the spellings to the children as follows:

1. Give the spelling number.

2. Say 'The word is...'.

3. Read the context sentence.

4. Repeat 'The word is...'.

Leave at least a 12-second gap between spellings.

At the end, re-read all 20 questions. Then say *This is the end of the test please put down your pen or pencil.*

Each correct answer should be awarded **1 mark**. For more information on marking this paper, please refer to page 82.

Spelling one: the word is **building**.

The new **building** was developing very quickly.

The word is **building**.

Spelling two: the word is **arrival**.

His parents were waiting for his flight's **arrival**.

The word is **arrival**.

Spelling three: the word is **perhaps**.

Perhaps we will be able to read the book again tomorrow.

The word is **perhaps**.

Spelling four: the word is **straight**.

A hexagon has six **straight** sides.

The word is **straight**.

Spelling five: the word is **question**.

The **question** was quite tricky but she managed to complete it.

The word is **question**.

Spelling six: the word is **amateur**.

She had been an **amateur** gymnast for a few years.

The word is **amateur**.

Spelling seven: the word is **attachment**.

Ben opened the **attachment** to the email, wondering what was inside it.

The word is **attachment**.

Spelling eight: the word is **conscious**.

She became **conscious** of lots of people looking at her.

The word is **conscious**.

Spelling nine: the word is **definitely**.

I will **definitely** see you tomorrow.

The word is **definitely**.

Spelling ten: the word is **opportunity**.

It was a fantastic **opportunity** and he wouldn't turn it down.

The word is **opportunity**.

Spelling eleven: the word is **existence**.

Some people believe in the **existence** of the Loch Ness monster.

The word is **existence**.

Spelling twelve: the word is **embarrassment**.

There was a lot of **embarrassment** when they arrived on the wrong day.

The word is **embarrassment**.

Spelling thirteen: the word is **language**.

They couldn't work out what **language** the children were speaking.

The word is **language**.

Spelling fourteen: the word is **stomach**.

He had **stomach** ache all morning.

The word is **stomach**.

Spelling fifteen: the word is **correspondence**.

The secretary had a lot of **correspondence** to deal with.

The word is **correspondence**.

Spelling sixteen: the word is **thorough**.

The doctor gave him a **thorough** examination.

The word is **thorough**.

Spelling seventeen: the word is **soldier**.

He joined the army to become a **soldier**.

The word is **soldier**.

Spelling eighteen: the word is **occupations**.

There is a wide choice of **occupations** for school leavers.

The word is **occupations**.

Spelling nineteen: the word is **pronunciation**.

The **pronunciation** of consonants is very different in Spanish.

The word is **pronunciation**.

Spelling twenty: the word is **especially**.

We are **especially** proud to announce the winner of the courtesy award.

The word is **especially**.

QUICK TESTS FOR SATs SUCCESS

BOOST YOUR CHILD'S CONFIDENCE WITH 10-MINUTE SATs TESTS

-  Bite-size mini SATs tests which take just 10 minutes to complete
- Covers key National Test topics
- Full answers and progress chart provided to track improvement
- Available for Years 1 to 6

Find out more at www.scholastic.co.uk